ENDORSEMENTS

"This book is definitely a must read for a new and existing landlord. I have been renting for over 30 years and found out information I was unaware of reading this book. The legal issues alone have changed so much I am redoing my lease, and my insurance. The book is easy to read. I will be recommending it to our local apartment association." Thank you!

Cindy Grode.

"If you own a home and have an extra bedroom and bathroom that you aren't using, and the thought of earning a steady income from renting these rooms interests you, then you will want to buy a copy of this book. This will serve you well as a comprehensive resource to know what it takes to rent out a part of your home."

Rosemarie Rossetti, Ph.D., President, Rossetti Enterprises Inc.

Quote from roommates

Sharing the house temporarily with Michelle was easy and affordable. I was able to come and go as I needed. A clothes washer and drier was conveniently located in the apartment, and more than enough room to keep my "stuff".

Steve B.

The room Michelle offered for rent came at the perfect time for me and was an extremely ideal situation. I was in the process of transferring within the company I work for and moving to an area which I was completely unfamiliar. Michelle offered a short term lease and the room came fully furnished, which worked out great as it gave me time to explore places to live and shop for a home to buy. I had a very positive experience renting from Michelle and it helped me out greatly in my transition to a new city.

Chris S., Nuclear Instrumentation Technician (4-17-17)

"As soon as I graduated from college, I got a job that required me to move to the Cleveland area. I had no friends, family, or connections to the area, and, as a single woman, was worried about finding safe and affordable housing. Discovering Michelle's ad on Craig's List was great! Her description and pictures of the living area were true to what I found, and her screening process was fair and straightforward. As a landlord, Michelle was wonderful! Having spent the majority of her life in the area, she was able to let me know the best parks, places to shop, and restaurants to try. She was always friendly, and worked with me to make sure we were both settling in to the new situation with open communication and a clear understanding of what was expected from both of us. It was a wonderful experience.

Kelsey G (4-21-17)

THE MONEY ROOM

MICHELLE MOORE BRADY

Published by Motivational Press, Inc.
1777 Aurora Road
Melbourne, Florida, 32935
www.MotivationalPress.com

Manufactured in the United States of America.

ISBN: 978-1-62865-438-7

Contents

Money Room

CHAPTER 1 - The Money Room

CHAPTER 2 - The Money Room

CHAPTER 3 - The Money Room

CHAPTER 4 - The Money Room

CHAPTER 5 - The Money Room

CHAPTER 6 - The Money Room

CHAPTER 7 - The Money Room

The Money Room

To the roommates I enjoyed, and those that provided valuable learning lessons this book helps you prevent!

THANKS

Too many people are involved to make a book effort come to completion. My list is longer yet special mention to:

- My parents, Kathy, Tom, Deb Wyckoff, my church family and many more. Special people who have supported my unique housing and especially listen to me when it was not going my way!

- Sandy Rozelman, Jeff Nischwitz and Diane Helbig who offered their publishing experience, suggestions and ideas that kept me from making mistakes. Rosemarie Rosetti who reviewed and endorsed the book, plus added research! Thanks!

- Mona Newbaucher and TL Champion who provided initial reviews, edits, recommendations and humor injections which made this book better.

Finally, thanks to Motivational Press who gave a first time author a chance!

DISCLOSURE

This book is based on the author's personal experience over 25 years renting to roommates and is not intended to be legal advice. Laws vary from state/province to country and this information is not, nor is it intended to be, legal advice. It is provided solely as the author's experience, as a guidebook, and to create awareness of common rental situations you might face. Someone planning to rent should do due-diligence in your geographical area.

Alias name vs. actual names are used especially where less-than-acceptable roommate stories are discussed.

Money Room

INTRODUCTION

My house has never been lonely. For over 30 years I have had various roommates as a strategic effort to increase income, share expenses, provide security vs living alone and barter for household maintenance. My experience began when I had roommates throughout college and I continued it when I owned a house. Renting my house helped me get out of debt until other good reasons for sharing my home emerged. When others found out about my roommate experience some began asking me advice. This book <u>The Money Room: create an income stream renting rooms</u> was created from long emails helping others figure out their roommate and rental situations.

Renting hasn't been entirely painless – there were some tough lessons! While I've benefited greatly from renting, I also learned from a couple negative situations. Stressful roommates I call "*bozos*" were a small number. There have been less than a half-dozen or so bozos and they do not outweigh the good roommate experiences. My hope is to share with you what I do to avoid bozos so you can duplicate the positive roommate outcomes sharing your house.

MY STORY

I intentionally became a landlord/roommate when I purchased and invested significant effort and funds to redesign a single-family home into a 3-person shared housing environment. Initially I rented to two roommates until I scaled back to just one.

A. Avoiding bankruptcy: Reducing debt was my primary motivation while renting rooms. Like many Americans I was illiterate about healthy financial management and made a lot of mistakes. By the year 2000 I was emerging from two financially-trying decades. I was struggling to manage debt from a myriad of sources including a failed-business, college student loan debt, medical debt, house and car debts, and normal living expenses. On top of the debt, I was beginning work in a new career field at an entry-level salary. By age 30 I was over $200,000 in debt. Several financial advisers thought the situation was hopeless and they all recommended filing bankruptcy.

As a faith-based person I felt strongly about not declaring bankruptcy without trying to pay the debt. I know a lot of people do declare bankruptcy and I fully understand that there are many reasons to make that decision. For me, however, my faith prompted me to first make a good effort to try and pay it off based on the belief that "nothing is impossible" with God. Armed with faith and willingness to be creative, I was ready to put forth an effort to pay off these obligations. I related to the quote "people run into debt and then have to crawl out" because it was now time for me to crawl out.

B. Renting created income: If I had any hope of getting out of debt I needed another reliable income source.

I was already working two jobs both full-time and part-time so I couldn't work more. Renting provided another income stream, shortened the time to become debt-free, and kept me out of bankruptcy without getting another job. Room rental rates in my area charge $400-600, so renting a fully-furnished place in the middle of this range at $500 proved to attract suitable clients and it has lasted 18 years! Renting rooms helped me finally gain some financial success, and it felt great rewriting my financial story!

C. House renovations: The reason I think that others can duplicate my efforts renting rooms is because my house is not unusual; it is a normal American home. It is a modest 1950's cookie-cutter-duplicated Bungalow in an older residential neighborhood. It had 1,500 square foot, two 12x12 bedrooms and an open upstairs bedroom, 1-1/2 baths, and a partially finished basement. The main bath was 4' x 8' and kitchen is 9x9 and both are very small by American new housing standards.

I redesigned this space to create three separate living areas doing the following:

- In the basement I essentially created an apartment. I took a large former family-room and installed a divider-wall with entry doors. This created both a bedroom and a living room. To comply with city codes I had to install a costly fire-escape window in the bedroom ($500); however, I reasoned it would only take one month of rent to pay off that investment. I then created a kitchenette with appliances near the stairwell, efficiently using a small space. I added a portable dishwasher next to the utility sink by the laundry. While we all share the laundry in the common area, this is my primary rental space in my home's lower level.

- Next I added bathrooms to my house. Through contractors I installed a completely new bathroom in the basement and expanded an upstairs 1/2-bath into a full bath, creating a master suite.

- The first-floor original two bedrooms and full-bathroom in the center were modified by adding a door to the entryway to section-it-off. This door created a living unit for another roommate that would share the original kitchen. One of the two bedrooms serves as that roommate's living room.

These renovations added value and they gave me two rental areas, including a new in-law suite. I furnished the entire place through inexpensive estate sales and offered my rental fully-furnished. This turned out to be a good decision as it attracted a niche-market.

The laundry is in the newly-created separated area and all household members use it, so it's not exclusive to the roommate. Because the home has shared areas

it is not legally considered a duplex but is classified as a "boarding house". Further because I'm an on-site-homeowner seeking a *'roommate'* there are fewer rules than for traditional landlords which I will discuss in this book.

D. Estimated investment: The home modifications I outlined required a $16,000 investment which I financed on credit cards. The largest single cost was $10,000 on the bathrooms. I calculated rental income would make the debt payment and hopefully break-even in 3-5 years and this occurred.

E. I found a niche market: I quickly found I that didn't like short-term rental. While Airnub, Airbnb and other internet sites has created a fad for this, I disliked quick turn-overs. It simply took too much effort to attract, interview, and screen potential roommates, as well as restore a unit to accept short-term rental. I found that I preferred renting at least three months at a time and set that as the lease minimum. I knew this was a good minimum when I still received interested potential roommate calls. I've had roommates who stayed for just the minimum three months to one that lasted four years.

I identified my niche market when out-of-state professionals working temporary contracts responded to my online ads (discussed in this book). They liked both the shorter-term lease and fully-furnished feature. They really liked that it was much less than the cost of our local Residence-inn and was homier. I began focusing my recruitment activity on these professionals. To drum up customers I reached out to local businesses, hospitals and colleges in an effort to find similar clients. This worked and I started to get roommate referrals without significant advertising.

Renting to professionals became a win-win per these former tenant testimonies:

- *The room Michelle offered for rent came at the perfect time for me and was an extremely ideal situation. I was in the process of transferring within the company I work for and moving to an area which I was completely unfamiliar. Michelle offered a short term lease and the room came fully furnished, which worked out great as it gave me time to explore places to live and shop for a home to buy. I had a very positive experience renting from Michelle and it helped me out greatly in my transition to a new city.*

Chris S., Nuclear Instrumentation
Technician (4-17-17)

- *"As soon as I graduated from college, I got a job that required me to move to the Cleveland area. I had no friends, family, or connections to the area, and, as a single woman, was worried about finding safe and affordable housing. Discovering Michelle's ad on Craig's List was great! Her description and pictures of the living area were true to what I found, and her screening process was fair and straightforward. It was a wonderful experience.*

Kelsie G. (4-21-17)

F. How renting rooms has helped me:

1. Roommates created an independent income stream that helped me:

   - Paid-off of my credit cards debts instead of declaring bankruptcy.

   - Improved my credit score and lowered my credit costs because of above.

- Afforded costly repairs when needed.

- Reduced mortgage debt by paying more on the mortgage bill.

- Created home equity. The lowered mortgage, my improved credit score, and the added-value home-renovations helped me obtain an attractive low-interest and tax-deductible home equity line, a more appealing credit source.

- Saved taxes because the U.S.A. tax law provides legitimate rental property deductions for a home-based business.

- Saved money and began an emergency fund.

- Covered housing costs during a time of extended unemployed. In 2014 during an economic downturn my job was eliminated. Roommates helped me meet my home expenses during unemployment.

2. Non-monetary benefits. While money was my main reason for sharing I also received secondary benefits including:

- Bartering. Roommates sometimes provided home maintenance (i.e., lawn cutting, pet care, moving heavy stuff, etc.) in exchange for rent reductions.

- Home security. A roommate provided added safety vs. living alone.

- Companionship. Most roommates were usually friendly and several times a long-term friendship was forged. While not all roommates were missed, many are people I enjoyed getting to know and remain in contact. A handful of the roommates are now life-long friends.

G. My experience can be your guide. Renting was definitely not stress-free. I encountered frustrations, compromises, property damages and learned many hard lessons. As mentioned at the beginning of this chapter there were a couple "bozos". The rest of this book is advice to help others duplicate the positive roommate outcomes and reduce potential bozos. My knowledge is not just experience-based. This book is supplemented by research and training provided by a local apartment association, accounting professionals, legal services, self-help law books and online resources. I look forward to helping you as I share my experiences.

Let's get started!

CHAPTER 1 - The Money Room

WHO MIGHT WANT TO SHARE A HOUSE AND WHY?

A. What types of people might want to consider house-sharing?

1. Mortgage-poor home-owners who use extra space to pay the mortgage and home improvements.

2. Senior citizens who have homes formerly occupied by children and whose rooms can be repurposed.

3. Disabled persons can enjoy both roommate income and bartered support for health or home care.

4. Single parents who can add income without working another job away from their children. Parents can gain both roommate income, potential childcare and perhaps a companion.

5. College students could consider providing their own housing by purchasing their own campus house, and then pay the bills with a roommate. At the same time they share and save on campus housing expenses, they are also building property equity. After college graduation when they sell the property, the proceeds could be used towards paying any student debt and they pocket the savings earned from providing their own campus housing.

6. A *"good Samaritan"* helping someone is great, but admirable unless they are taken advantage-of while doing a good deed? You may wish to help a young person, someone divorcing, unemployed, low-income, single-mom, college student, a senior on a fixed income, someone managing a health issue, etc. Before bringing someone into your home, you can use this book to clarify your charity limits and expectations.

7. Someone living near a college campus, a large business, a popular attraction (i.e., amusement park, museum) who sees an opportunity renting to a ready roommate source.

8. Anyone seeking to get-out-of debt, increase income and create an income stream they control!

Of course there may be other reasons I haven't considered and I welcome hearing why you've picked-up this book. You can write me at <u>MBrady@SageForward.com</u> to share your story.

B. Current financial climate and trends: Challenging economic times are the primary motivation towards creative income stream development such as roommate and housing-sharing trends!

1. Studies are showing that 40-50% of Americans are on the verge of financial disaster and have no back-up plan:

   - According to the results of a national survey *"one in three Americans would be unable to make their mortgage or rent payment beyond one month if they lost their job"*. [Reference:

http://mandelman.ml-implode.com/2011/10/
only-one-paycheck-away-from-disaster-no-
kidding-really-go-figure/, *September 2011*]

- According to Tony Robbins in <u>Money</u> *"77% of Americans -- three of every four people -- say they have financial worries, but only 40% report having any kind of spending or investments plan. One in three baby boomers have less than $1,000 saved!* [Reference: Anthony Robbins. Money, Master the Game: 7 Simple Steps to Financial Freedom. Simon and Shuster, 2014. pp6.]

- According to The Huffington Post *"nearly Half Of American Households Are 1 Emergency Away From Financial Disaster, Report Finds"* [Reference: The Huffington Post by <u>Jillian Berman</u>, Posted: 01/30/2013 12:01 am EST Updated: 01/30/2013 4:35 pm EST. http://www.huffingtonpost.com/2013/01/30/financial-emergency-report_n_2576326.html]

2. Studies are showing shared housing is a trend:

- *"To manage high rent, baby boomers are increas-*

ingly open to living with roommates. Numerous boomers are using SpareRoom to find roommates," said Hutchinson, *noting spikes in major housing markets such as Dallas, Los Angeles, San Francisco, Seattle, and Philadelphia. Interestingly, it's not just money concerns that motivate boomers to take on a roomie or two. Sometimes, social factors are at play"* [Reference: CNBC reports on August 19, 2016. http://www.cnbc.com/2017/02/06/living-like-millennials-ba-by-boomers-are-renting-paying-off-debt-and-have-roommates.html]

- *"Although renting out a room in your home may seem like a drastic measure, it's actually becoming more commonplace as homeowners look for creative ways to help make ends meet. One of the top 5 things you can do to earn additional money is monetize your spare room"* [Reference: Matthew Ong, September 29, 2014, US News and World Report]

- *Even on TV, from The Odd Couple to The Big Bang Theory, renters have always known that the easiest way to save on housing costs was to share a place – even if certain roommates drive you a little bit crazy. In America's biggest rental markets, a renter can save on average 13% of his or her income by getting a roommate. While splitting a room with roommate(s) will save you money, the benefits of sharing a living space vary from city to city, home to home.* [Reference: TRULIA: Room For Rent: Where Getting A Roommate Pays Off the Most by Mark Uh, Feb 23, 2017, found at https://www.trulia.com/blog/trends/room-for-rent/]

- The U.S.A. Census Bureau reported "the number of unrelated adults living in someone else's home jumped 12% between 2008 and 2010, to 7.3 million. That includes roommates sharing rentals as well as adults renting out rooms in other people's homes".* [Reference: Should you rent out a room? Liz Weston, MSN MONEY, http://money.msn.com/home-loans/should-you-rent-out-a-room-weston.aspx, 9/12/2011 6:21 PM ET by Liz Weston.]

This article studied people sharing housing and how much money might be earned renting across the United States. This chart is a great example of the financial benefit sharing housing costs in major US cities (permission to use):

[Reference: TRULIA, Room For Rent: Where Getting A Roommate Pays Off the Most by Mark Uh, Feb 23, 2017, found at https://www.trulia.com/blog/trends/room-for-rent/]

C. Non-financial motivators: As mentioned in my introductory story, I benefited from more than the added income provided by my roommates. Renting can provide non-monetary benefits such as:

1. Bartering/exchange: Someone could exchange housing for maintenance services:

- Home maintenance: A room can be bartered for services such as odd jobs, seasonal house maintenance (i.e., lawn-care, winterizing, etc.), pet care, etc.

- In-home care: Baby boomers are the largest over 50 population living on this planet and they are aging. The elderly might be able to exchange housing for live-in health-care or services.

2.   Security: Someone living alone may feel safer with another person on the premises. Perhaps you travel often and having a roommate provides security for an otherwise empty house.

3.   Companionship: Single people living alone may not want a romantic relationship but might want a companion.

- CNBC reports on August 19, 2016 *"millennials choose to live with others for social reasons and boomers do the same. In fact we found that many boomers choose to share living accommodations even though they can afford to live alone."* (Found at: http://www.cnbc.com/2017/02/06/living-like-millennials-baby-boomers-are-renting-paying-off-debt-and-have-roommates.html).

I've enjoyed both the financial support and all the listed non-financial benefits having roommates. While my roommates provided me with funds, I also enjoyed the added security having them in my home and many became friends which I stay in contact.

If you did not find your reason please write me so that I can expand the list!

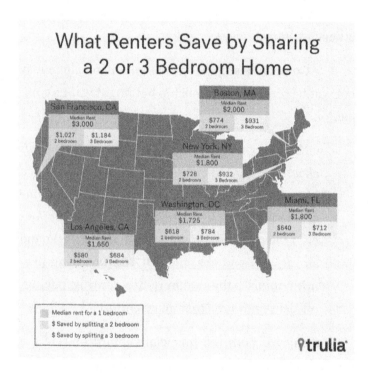

CHAPTER 2 - The Money Room

HOUSE SET-UP & ACCEPTABLE SITUATIONS

This chapter raises questions about the actual rental space you're offering and how much of your space your roommates will use and what situations you will accept. Let's discuss both your house set-up and some roommate/sharing decisions you will need to make.

1. Do you have a separate space that is desirable and rentable? Let's start with the most basic space questions -- how separate is your rental area from your personal areas? The ideal situation is a completely separate guest house, a garage apartment or an in-law suite with a separate entrance, utilities, kitchen, bath, bedroom, living room, and

parking. If you do not have the luxury of a completely separate unit, how much can you separate inside a shared property?

2. Do you have a separate rentable private bedroom? If you cannot provide a bedroom that is separate then you have a greater need to ensure that your roommate is someone you like, trust, and can tolerate in close-confinement.

   - My story: Personally I would not share a bedroom with a roommate; however, I was told a story by a roommate who viewed such a place. The potential landlord had simply strung a curtain in the bedroom to create a divided section. The potential roommate didn't want to share a bedroom and ended up renting with me for the private bedroom.

3. Do you have a separate bathroom to offer? Bathroom sharing is highly personal. Sharing requires working out issues of privacy, cleanliness, scheduling, storage separation of personal items, shared use of products (i.e., toiletries, towels, etc.), clear discussion of privacy requirements, and perhaps a greater need for likeability of the other person.

4. Do you have a separate living room to offer? If not have you considered privileges using your space? If you share your living room, you may have to clarify and compromise sharing issues such as entertainment equipment, programs viewed, hours, and volume, etc.?

- My story: My roommate has their own living room. I still hear noise sometimes from their TV and music but I definitely prefer it to sharing my space and entertainment/relaxation area.

5. Do you have a separate kitchen to offer or will you extend shared kitchen privileges? A separated kitchen is ideal but there are other issues to clarify:

A. Clean-up is more of an issue if you share a kitchen or see the roommates' messes:

- My stories: I had one roommate that made pumpkin beer. The process was an all-day affair that made a huge mess throughout the common area and laundry, preventing me from using it. He often took several days and prompting to get it cleaned back up. We had several conversations about cleaning it up more timely and extended efforts of this kind became a new cleanliness element I tolerated having this roommate.

B. Food and cost-sharing. Consider whether you are going to share food (i.e., spices, oil, etc.) or separate food entirely. Also consider what you will do if food or products you purchased become missing and you suspect a roommate took it.

C. Split the cost of items equally that you both use, such as paper towels, soap, etc.

D. Storage of food. Can you provide food separation? I provide my roommate an exclusive storage cabinet for their use and I store food in other storage cabinets. In the refrigerator, sharing reduces food quantity purchases and we attempt to split that space equally.

E. Scheduling time. What if you both want to use the kitchen at the same time? When you have roommates, having the kitchen to yourself is not always possible.

F. Appliances plugged-in. Do you mind if things are left running for a long-period, such as a fan, a coffee pot, etc.? Due to a family coffee-pot fire, I do not like leaving small appliances plugged-in all day (i.e., Keurig coffee pot, toaster oven or heaters) and I ask my roommates to unplug these appliances.

G. Breakage. Roommates may not take as much care of property as you. How will you handle breakage, repairs or loss replacement?

- My story: I have designated dishes and cooking pans that roommates use. This occurred after a roommate ruined a $50 Cuisinart Omelet pan cooking a boned steak on it. If you have to share, you may want to provide lesser-valued items.

H. Cooking produces both messes and smells.

- Other stories, I had a roommate that liked to cook strong food with aromatic smells that lingered for days. I had another roommate that baked for every holiday and during these holiday projects overtook the kitchen for days.

6. Do you have a separate and private entrance? Several issues occur with the roommate that does not have a separate entrance:

a) Security: If someone can access your area, security issues increase.

b) Interaction increases as you will probably regularly see each other.

- My story: I love having separate entrances. In my early years of renting I started out having two roommate (one 1st floor and one in the lower-level apartment). The 1st floor roommate shared my entrance. I rarely saw the roommate with the separate entrance because we can come and go separately but the one with the shared entrance I had to see interact with more often. With separate entrances seeing each other is rarer and less interaction is needed and definitely preferable.

7. Will you set rules for common area access? A common area is a public space that everyone can access. If you have a common area that you do not want used, then this need to be clarified, such as:

A. Laundry facilities: The concerns that may need to be discussed:

- When can the facilities be used? How early or late can someone use the facilities?

- Is there a separated storage area for detergent and laundry products?

- Will you charge for the use of the machines? Some owners install a coin-operated units.

- What about the care, cleanliness and condition of the machine? Sharing your maintenance expectations may be required. For instance, since it's a fire hazard to not clean out the dryer vent, I ask this to be done every use. Another example, one of my roommates overloaded the machine and could have resulted in breakage, so I provide recommendations about overloading it and why not to do this.

- Do you have things you don't want laundered in your home-machines? For instance, will you allow large comforters or dirty rugs that might deteriorate to be washed in your machine? What about heavily soiled, oily or smelly work-clothes that leave behind a residue which affects future wash-loads?

B. Parking, Driveway, and Garage:

- Where do you want your roommate to park? Many cities have limits to street parking and you'll want to communicate those laws. If parking occurs in a shared driveway, you may need to clarify specific parking locations/spots?

- What about non-working vehicles?

- My story: one roommate wanted to park a non-functional car in the driveway indefinitely and I had to deny the request. Not only was there limited space in the driveway but city ordinances do not allow long-term parking of disabled cars. It's a good idea to make decisions about this in advance and communicate it to a future roommate.

- Can you provide garage parking? If you share a garage, it's worth discussing how to park, if you will secure other items stored, etc.

- What about seasonal changes? A winter area deals with snow accumulation which affects parking spaces and snow-plowing. My snowy city allows no street parking after 2" snow accumulation. In summer we need to allow landscapers access past parked cars. These are things you might need to communicate to your roommates.

- What do you want done if the roommate leaves for an extended period and the car remains? Do you want to request the keys if moving the car becomes necessary?

C. Storage of property:

- Do you have items in the rooms that you are able and willing to store elsewhere? What about storing the roommates' items? How much stuff will you allow them to bring into your house? Too many items storage in a unit can create a fire-hazard.

- My story: I had roommates ask me to remove things from their rooms; however, I often struggled finding a place to put it and had to set limits about taking property out of the rooms. For example one roommate brought estate furniture in and wanted me to remove my items. I refused and discussed with her that I provided the room fully-furnished and her items had to remain minimal. I do remove knick-knacks and small items that I can store in the garage.

D. Sporting equipment, hot tub or pool or other expensive items: do you want roommates using it? If yes, consider:

- Liability: It's recommended that you talk to your insurance company about the liability you incur by having a roommate use your equipment.

- Safety concerns need to be addressed regarding your expectations, especially if there are any potential risks. Something as simple as someone falling off the equipment or falling down and or injuring themselves becomes your problem when it occurs on your property.

- What if the equipment breaks during their use? Will you seek money for repairs?

- Do you want them to clean anything after usage?

- What if they are using it when you want to do so? Does it need to be scheduled?

- Is there a cost involved in using it and do you want roommates to share it?

- My story: For a while I had a swimming pool. I made roommates sign a *'use-at-own-risk'* clause before using my swimming pool, releasing me if they are injured because there is greater risk associated with a swimming pool. I eventually dismantled the pool.

Contrary to this, I allowed roommates to use my treadmill without providing this release form.

8. Charges for shared utilities: Unless you have the luxury of a completely separate rental space with its own water-electric-gas and other utility meters separated, you may want to consider the cost of utilities. Will you pass these costs on to the room-mate? There are two ways to pass on the costs:

A. Calculate the actual costs and collect the utility percentage the renter pays every month.

B. Calculate an average utility cost and include that amount into the rent.

- My story: Initially I tried splitting all utilities as a separate bill. Roommates disliked two bill sets of paying rent and then separately paying utilities and claimed it was challenging to budget the varying utility expense. I evaluated the average utility costs and added it into a flat-rent rate. To control excessive usage, I kept a clause in my lease that if utilities exceed norms I will ask everyone to split that overage. Usually this comes up only when we are using more of our utilities due to extreme weather (i.e., air conditioning or heat) and discuss keeping utility usage down or sharing the premium cost.

Additional utilities decisions:

A. Internet: Personally I don't think you could rent without providing internet access. I provide this as an included charge for my roommates by creating a separate password for their use.

B. Cable or paid TV: Per above, I provide the internet, but not cable. Instead I provide roommates each with a DVD player and access to my Netflix account.

- My story: I let a roommate install cable. Six months later when he moved out, the cable company wanted to charge my property address an early-disconnect-fee. They also wouldn't take down the dish. I learned the dish-install damaged my roof and the cable company refused to cover the cost of the repair. I now avoid these frustrations by simply not providing something that can have unknown costs.

C. Phone service: Because of the potential for abuse I do not include a phone with rentals.

- My story: I started out providing a phone but withdrew it after two negative experiences. One out-of-state roommate made long distance calls and didn't want to cover them. Another roommate ran up the phone bill by 300% using fee-based phone features. Fortunately the phone company both negotiated the charges and blocked future use. After that experience I stopped providing phone service and it has not been an issue since everyone has a personal cell phone.

9. Other issues to consider:

A. Insurance: I strongly recommend you talk to your insurance company about liabilities and get added coverage. You as a landlord will be held accountable if someone gets hurt on your property, does damage, etc.

- My story: My insurance company advised me to raise my home-owners policy to cover a potential roommate lawsuit.. They also advised me to add a renter's insurance recommendation to my lease. To my knowledge no roommate has obtained renters insurance, but I did my part to warn that there could be consequences by not having it.

B. City laws: Does your city have any landlord-renter rules (i.e., fire prevention)? To prevent problems, check out your city and state rules.

- My story: My city has landlord laws but roommate laws were considered separate from their jurisdiction. They classified my property as a *"boarding house"* and it would only fall within their consideration if I didn't occupy it as an owner. As a prevention they offered to do an initial voluntary rental inspection for city code violations and I accepted. That inspection produced recommendations for extra fire-alarms which I installed, but otherwise my city is not involved.

Conclusion of this chapter: we considered your property and rental issues to consider before opening your home to roommates. Next we'll discuss the mental preparation factors considering opening your home to roommates.

CHAPTER 3 - The Money Room

MENTAL LANDLORD PREPARATION

Are you ready to be a landlord and roommate? A friend said "I *bet you need several personal traits that enable you share your home successfully*? Reflecting on this I couldn't agree more! I've learned that success comes from clearly setting expectations and immediately confronting potential issues after establishing a mutually respectful relationship.

This chapter reviews what situations you will accept (i.e., guests, pets, children, etc.). While *Fair Housing Laws* (this refers to United States anti-discrimination laws) apply for many situations (such as you cannot discriminate based on color or religion), as a homeowner-occupant seeking a *roommate* you can set certain conditions about who can share your personal home *with you*. The rights of a private homeowner sharing their home allow for choices in a couple areas, as long as you are consistent. The key here is that you must be consistent in your approach to be legal. Let's review these situations and the decisions you need to make.

Here are some thoughts to consider before taking in your first roommate!

1. Can you be firm about rent collection? The demand for on-time rent payment, late-fees enforcement, and pursuit of eviction if rent is not paid is the toughest issue that landlords experience. I've not met a landlord who didn't state that rent-collection was their #1 problem area. Early-on other landlords encouraged me to view renting as a strict business relationship. Most landlords agree that you cannot be soft on roommates because this will continuously occur. I've heard multiple landlord stories from who didn't evict upon non-payment who ended up housing someone three or more months free.

Here's a perspective from a landlord who has rented their home to people for over 30 years.

- *"I completely agree with NOT allowing a renter to stay due to sob-stories. I just sued a roommate who lived in one of my rentals. She said she had cancer and was behind on rent due to undergoing chemo. I couldn't bring myself to kick her out with cancer so I covered her rent for 6 months. She took a new job and signed a promissory note to pay everything off by within a specific due date. On that due date she instead moved-out without telling us! We tracked her down and filed against her and won - she was a no show in court. Despite winning, I haven't collected. We have to continue efforts to collect. The nicer you are - it sets up a false sense they can take advantage of you. I would stress two week limit".*

Cindy Grode

The good news is that in over 30 years of roommates I've only had to evict only four roommates due to failure-to-pay. In the next chapter I discuss several lessons-learned in Chapter 4 and the rent policies I set up and enforced to prevent rent issues.

2. Can you maintain a business-only relationship with a person living in your home? I've found it best to remain business-like and only slightly-involved in tenant lives in order to maintain clear boundaries. As a faith-based person I'd like to be clear that being *"business-like"* doesn't mean non-friendly. In fact I am still friendly, making gestures such as inviting roommates to share meals, chats, and occasional social events while still maintaining a clear business relationship, as demonstrated by this quote:

- *"As soon as I graduated from college, I got a job that required me to move to the Cleveland area. I had no friends, family, or connections to the area, and, as a single woman, was worried about finding safe and affordable housing. As a landlord, Michelle was wonderful! Having spent the majority of her life in the area, she was able to let me know the best parks, places to shop, and restaurants to try. She was always friendly, and worked with me to make sure we were both settling in to the new situation with open communication and a clear understanding of what was expected from both of us. It was a wonderful experience.*

Kelsie G. (4-21-17)

This former roommate quote demonstrates that a friendly business-relationship does not mean unfriendly or cold. It does mean not becoming too involved just in case you are placed in the position of evicting due to a contract breach (i.e., failure to pay).

3. Can you be firm confronting interpersonal confrontation? While roommates bring the long list of benefits, there's a tradeoff in things you manage, tolerate and perhaps endure. I enjoyed the benefits of having roommates, but I also found that roommates could be a nuisance too. Several took a lot of energy to tolerate. You need to consider how you are going to handle the issues that arise from having another person in your space (i.e., noise, uncleanliness, accidental breakage, intruding on your time, etc.). While I discuss my expectations about common issues in my lease, roommates always required a necessary tolerance. When prob-

lems arise I found it best to be direct and quickly confront as an effort to prevent reoccurrence. In chapter 4 I describe the policies I created to help you design your own.

4. Are you willing to repair your house? I rarely have a roommate who didn't do minor damage, and occasionally significant damage occurred.

- My story: A roommate had different cleanliness standards than I did. She stored her property literally in hundreds of plastic bags and piled them 3'-5' high on top each other throughout her unit. At first the bags attracted bugs and required professional pest-fumigation. The bags also created a fire safety and access issue and I felt compelled to issue warnings to clear a safe-pathway. After several warnings and continual non-compliance, I asked her to leave. Upon her leaving I found significant real damage because the bags leaked something that left dark mold imbedded in formerly beautiful 55 year-old hardwood floors. I had to cover the repair cost and the delay re-renting the unit while it was repaired. Even though the repaired hardwood floors looked nice, replacing them wiped out any profit. Attempts to recover the money failed because she was insolvent.

Damage to this degree was rare since most roommates want their security deposit returned. Extensive damage is not the norm but it is always a possibility when a stranger is using your property.

5. What will you set as a security deposit? How much you can charge is a legally-controlled issue and you should investigate your city and state rules; however, you should definitely charge a security deposit. A deposit helps you protect your property because roommates want to get their money back. While there are laws regarding this, I think you should set it high, usually as much as a month's rent. Some landlords collect both the first and last month rent and the security, but I found that was a lot of money up-front for many to provide. Most landlords feel that a security deposit also helps you screen for a roommate who has the financial resources to pay the bill.

- My Story: My rent is $550 and I set my security deposit at $400 which is the norm in my area and collected the first month and security together upon move-in. Sometimes people seeking roommate housing have financial problems. I have been both asked to waive my security deposit and pay it in installments. I never waived the security, but for the two roommates that I let pay the security in two installments, both had issues paying rent throughout their stay. My limited experience is that someone able to pay the security and first month rent has less likelihood of future rent payment issues.

6. Will you take couples or children? This is also a legally-controlled issue, but roommate rules allow a resident landlord a choice about couples when seeking a roommate *if* you are consistent. *Fair Housing Laws* prevent discrimination based on race, sexuality, religion, couples, children, etc.. An on-site landlord looking for a roommate does <u>not have to take multiple people,</u> which means you have a choice regarding couples and kids. You still cannot discriminate based on race, religion, sexual preference;

however, how many people you accept is an option <u>if you always and only seek to rent to just one person</u> <u>and</u> remain a live-on-site occupant-owner. If you accept a couple or child even once, you would set a precedence for couples and then would not be allowed to discriminate against future couples or children based on this precedence.

Keep in mind that not renting to couples <u>doesn't</u> <u>mean a single-status</u> person. The United States financial climate has created a challenging employment culture where many people have to seek and accept work out-of-state. In fact, this group of people turned out to be my niche market:

- My story: My best roommates were often married and temporarily working in my state and needing furnished short-term housing. I estimate at least 65% of my roommates were married contractors working out-of-state and leaving behind their family in their home state. These roommates worked all week and then drove home to be with their families on weekends.

My best example of this roommate type was my Navy Seal roommate. His wife and small children were in Georgia while he worked a short-term project at the Veterans Administration Hospital near my home. He worked three weeks and took off a week to go home for seven months. He filled his evenings at dinner-time Skyping with is very young children. The arrangement worked for this family short-term.

In another example, Tim, a married computer contractor, accepted a short-term contract at a local company installing a computer program modification. He then moved-on to another state to do the same thing. I became a housing reference for him as he sought similar accommodations in other locations.

If your property accommodates couples then consider addressing multiple cars and parking, relationship issues, joint lease agreement making both parties responsible, running a dual-person screening including both individuals and obtaining both I.D's to hold each one accountable, and what will you do if they get pregnant while living with you? Similar considerations arise with children including added wear and tear, play areas, safety elements, etc.

- My story: Since I have only sought an individual roommate, I do not have advice or experiences to share regarding couples or kids. I've only sought housing a single individual roommate for many reasons, mostly space and cars and it's a lot less effort to deal with just one roommate. I once considered a missionary couple coming off the mission-field to help them; however, since I was very concerned about establishing a precedent and having to take future couples, I was glad when they found another place.

7. What will be your guest policy? A guest is a reasonable request; however, will you set limits regarding a guest stay? A few concerns arise with guests including parking spaces, communicating security expectations (i.e., will you allow more keys to be made for guests), added expenses, and what will you do if the guest doesn't leave?

  - My story: My guest policy has worked well. I allow overnight and temporary guests at the roommates' discretion as long as the guest stays a few days and they notify me. I ask for notice so that I'm not surprised to meet another person in my house. The notification can be as simple as a text that *a friend will be here this weekend* without further communication needed. I don't mind a temporary or even regular guest, but I ask roommates to limit guests to a couple days or discuss it. I ask for the roommate to not provide additional keys for security protection of us all and to be present when their guest is in the house.

Two examples of good outcomes with the guest policy: 1) A roommate had four older grandchildren visit for a summer week vacation. We agreed on a plan to accommodate the children in the house (including using my living room space for them to sleep), and we agreed upon an increased rent amount to cover the week's added expenses. The visit went well. 2). Several of my out-of-state contractors entertained spouses over long weekends without issue. One roommates spouse and adult son visited so they could look for houses over a week and the visit went smoothly.

Two examples where my guest-policy did not work out: 1). One prospective roommate wanted her mother to live with us for a four month extended visit; however, she objected to paying additional rent. This prospective roommate chose to move elsewhere. 2). Another roommate allowed a boyfriend to move-in, a man which I had neither met during our interview-stage, nor would have allowed to move-in. I wasn't introduced to him formally; instead I met him in-passing me one morning as he was leaving. I became very uncomfortable with him when he rudely refused to speak to me. The second time I met him he behaved the same. Since I found him to be disrespectful, this caused me increasing unease having this complete stranger in my home. I began to get angry when I saw his car in my driveway every single night. I started discussing it with the roommate, yet after three increasing stronger discussions in two weeks about lowering her guest occupancy, nothing changed. I then posted a written warning with the lease she signed, highlighting the guest-policy section. Within that week they decided to get an apartment together and I let her break the lease (she was moving-out earlier than the minimum time requirement). I probably would have had to evict her otherwise, so I was relieved when she moved-out amicably. This was an instance where the guest policy was not respected and it caused strain.

8. How much socializing do you want with your roommate? How social do you want to be with your roommates? Do you want to spend extended amounts of time together? Do you want to attend social event together? Do you want to offer rides and grocery shopping or other services?

- My story: I choose to remain friendly but separate from roommates. Even though I communicate this at move-in to roommates, I did have one that wanted more social interaction than I could provide and it caused an issue. The roommate was a sweet elderly lady who simply needed companionship. Unfortunately I was overburdened working both a full-time and part-time job and I simply couldn't offer the amount of socializing time she wanted. She followed me around to talk to me despite my demanding schedule and it prevented me getting things done. To avoid her so I could work,

I ended up becoming a prisoner in my room. I tried talking to her about my lack of availability, yet it persisted. Eventually she moved near a senior center which met her needs better.

This story above the reason your social interaction expectations need clarified. I now discuss socializing in the interview stage.

9. Will you allow smoking, drugs, and parties?

   a. Smoking: What is your position on smoking in your home? If you want non-smoking, have you set up a designated place outside your home to smoke?

   b. Drug policy: Drugs may be an obvious illegal and not-acceptable issue; however you need to define your policy up-front what you will do if suspected or observed.

   c. Party policy: Do you want to let roommates have a large group gathering or party?

   • My story: Upon arriving home one day I smelled marijuana in my backyard. A college student roommate was home with his girl-friend. I didn't see the usage but it was definitely near the proximity of my house. I suspected them. Since I didn't see it I didn't directly confront and instead inferred meaning by stating: *"someone smoked marijuana nearby. Since I fear attracting police to my home, did you see anyone nearby today"*? This approach avoided direct accusation and reminded if they were the ones that did smoke nearby, they were to move the behavior off my property. It never happened again.

10. Will you take pets? Will you allow a cat, dog, caged animals, exotic animals, snakes, rodents, certain size of animals, etc.? If yes, how many animals will you allow? Does size matter? There's a big difference between a Terrier and a Rottweiler, and a cat vs five of them. Many landlords allow pets but charge a premium security deposit and a premium monthly rent. The assumption is that increased maintenance and repair of the unit will be required, (such as new carpet) after an animal has been present.

- My story: I do not allow roommates to bring animals although I have been asked to consider dogs and cats and I have refused. I already have two cats and I was both concerned about pet interaction, sanitization and future roommate allergies, and damage. Due to these concerns, my policy is to take no additional pets. This policy has not prevented finding roommates.

11. How will you do record-keeping? You need records for roommate billing, income reporting and for claiming taxes and tax-deductions. There are several things you will need to document in order to claim tax deductions including roommate rent records, expenses and tax-deductible items. I created a system that was simple and easy using a 1-page roommate income/bill Excel file. The form both records rent records and serves as the roommate's receipt:

	Roommate Name		

MONTHLY RENTAL info

	Reg rent	PAID	credit	notes credit
January	$____	$____	$____	Maintenance discount?
YEAR END =	Total Income $____	Deduction $____	$____	

Items I record for tax deductions include total utilities; home labor costs (i.e., contractors, property and lawn care); home maintenance and improvements; purchases for the rental; any other roommate expenses, such as repairs; and deductions/bartering exchange that reduce taxable income. In Chapter 7 we'll review tax advantages renting and having a home-based business.

CHAPTER 4 - The Money Room

DEFINING YOUR ROOMMATE AND RENTAL POLICIES

This chapter is about creating a cohabitation success plan and avoiding preventable conflicts. Throughout my many renting years I created and redesigned a *'roommate understanding'* document that communicates my expectations to prospective roommates. I believe having written expectations up-front helped ensure compatibility and prevent issues. Whatever your rules, I recommend you also commit them in writing and provide roommates a copy so they are not forgotten.

While I strongly advise setting clear expectations, I once read a rental guidebook that recommended not setting rules because, they asserted, such rules prevent individual freedoms and flexibility. I couldn't disagree more because for me having rules reduces stress. There's stress enough allowing a near-stranger to share space. Contrary to the few-rules advice I find having written rules at the prospective roommate interview allows them to determine if they will be comfortable with these expectations. Many former roommates have told me that they appreciated the detailed expectations I presented because they wanted the same type of roommate.

The items you may want to consider while creating your policies and expectations:

1. Rent Payment Policy: Collecting rent is *the* most challenging issue landlord's face. Every landlord needs to decide how they will respond when a roommate does not pay their rent on-time. The need to both clearly outline and enforce rental policies is the most stressful and problematic rental issue.

A. <u>Be firm about rent</u>: My advice to a new landlord was learned the hard way. I started out being lenient and not enforcing immediate consequences for late rent. This invited additional instances of late rent every time. While I want to keep roommates, I do not want to keep non-paying ones. My experience could have been less stressful had I been firm at the beginning about a late rent policy.

- My story: The rent learning experience: In my early rental experience I allowed a roommate who was financially in trouble to pay late and ended up with long-term problems. He was a nice guy who became unemployed after a few months. Instead of his *John Hancock* signature on a check his signature was on pieces of paper....long notes explaining why he wasn't paying. The first time he didn't pay rent on-time I listened sympathetically to his difficulties. He had some of the rent and he promised to pay within a few days. I accepted partial rent and agreed to a new date for the rest without taking any other action (i.e., with no late fee consequences).

After three or so continued issues, I consulted my Legal Shield attorney for advice (I discuss using attorneys in Chapter 7). Unfortunately I wasn't aware that accepting that first late-rent and not enforcing late fees had set a legal precedence. I learned that accepting rent late even one time changed the lease terms and creates a new precedent which could be difficult to reverse. My attorney advised me to begin applying the lease's outlined consequences and crate a clear late-acceptance policy. The next time I was ready with a 3-day eviction notice and a late fee (I asked $10 a day). My Apartment Association taught me about the eviction process. Normal landlords also post a 3-day eviction warning; however, for them it is the date they can begin filing formal eviction through their courts. A court eviction can take 30-days to evict. For a roommate, I ask roommates to begin seeking other accommodations after 3-days late.

This roommate lived with me for four years and he paid both the rent and late-fees on multiple occasions. By posting a 3-day eviction warning I elevated paying rent to top priority. While I liked this guy, I did not like the late rent and he wasn't my roommate so I could support *him*.

Another landlord stated how strongly she agreed with not being soft-hearted about roommate failure-to-pay.

- *"I completely agree with NOT allowing a renter to stay due to sob-stories. I will say after 30 years of doing this only a handful ever pay what they owe".*

  Cindy Grode

B. <u>Set clear rent expectations</u>: My early experience of NOT having a clear-rent policy ended up creating an adversarial relationship which I quickly corrected going forward with all future tenants. Today I begin every roommate relationship stating that the number one priority is collecting money and that our roommate relationship is a *pay-to-stay* one. We can be friendly but if they don't have money to pay on rent day, they need to move-out in 3-days. In three of the four instances these failure-to-pay roommates quickly lined up alternative housing. One took three weeks to fully move out (she had moved out already but left things behind). I'm happy to report I did not have to take any of them to court!

C. <u>Rent is a legislated issue</u>: I was surprised to learn through the Apartment Association that a court is generally uninterested in the reasons a person doesn't pay. The stories that might make a landlord feel sympathetic are not usually listened to by a Court unless there are extenuating circumstances (i.e., if there's a dispute with a landlord who has done something wrong, such as not provided essential emergency maintenance). Simple *"failure to pay"* provides objective eviction grounds and the court is most likely to issue an eviction based solely on unpaid rent. Further the landlord must also comply with these laws. The court expects you to evict for non-payment and quickly. I heard one story of a court magistrate berating a landlord for not evicting someone that hadn't paid for three months. The landlord was being sympathetic (like I was with my first roommate), but the Court magistrate actually yelled at them saying that approach was no way to run a business!

I recommend you investigate these resources before designing your late rent policy:

- The statutes in your state and city: You could access and review these rules by visiting your city offices.

- An attorney: I'll talk about this in Chapter 7 but I had my lease reviewed by Legal Shield, a pre-paid legal service (because I like them so much I signed up to tell others about it. Check it out at *www.MichelleBrady.legalshieldassociate.com*). A Legal Shield attorney confirmed my lease met state laws. This attorney also helped when I consulted them about issues.

- An Apartment Association: they help with credibility, advice and support. Most states and major cities have a landlord association or apartment association. Joining one provides education, referrals, service discounts, comraderies, and problem-solutions. Mine helped me identify a tenant screening resource that I discuss in chapter 5.

D. <u>Late rent consequences</u>: here are some late rent components to consider including in your policy:

1. Late-fees: The goal of a late fee is to prohibit a future occurrence by applying consequences. I recommend charging a high enough amount to deter occurrence. I charge $10 a day per a Legal Shield attorney recommendation.

2. Another landlord shared with me their approach encouraging on-time payment. They list their rent amount including a *discount* for being on-time. Instead of charging a late-fee they have a per day rent amount with the late-fee included. The approach reframes the penalty viewpoint by showing the discounted on-time-price as a reward. To further encourage on-time payment they offer a 1-year no-late-rent bonus of $25-50.00 discount or a free promotional item. For instance the landlord buys reasonably priced flat-screens or other appealing small appliances as these bonus items. The cost is absorbed and the happy tenant celebrates their on-time rent annually.

3. Posted warnings: The laws may vary by city and state and I designed mine based on my apartment association and Legal Shield attorney advice.

- At the end of 24-hours I post a legal 3-day eviction-warning notice.

- At the end of the 3-days my city recommends beginning formal court eviction proceedings and posting an eviction in-process notice. If you choose to formally file you will have to go to your city court and file the appropriate eviction-forms at day #4. There are fees and processes involved and you might want to consult legal advice.

As already stated, I never had to do go to court. Each of my few eviction requests were accepted by roommates either moved out within 15 days to avoid court.

E. <u>Avoid court</u>: To date I have not had to formally file court eviction documents because each roommate moved out. Based on attorney advice I consulted I was advised to avoid court if possible due to these reasons:

1. Costs: courts cost incurred include filing fees and time.

2. Attorney: you may need to consult an attorney and incur costs for that advice until you learn to do an eviction yourself.

3. Time: it's time consuming to complete the process, obtain and attend a court date and wait your turn, present and defend your situation, and get a judges' decision and finalize the paperwork and costs.

4. Delays eviction: you place the eviction date in the hands of the court instead of between you and the roommate

5. Requires explanations: you are placed in a position of presenting your roommate situation to strangers, to defend yourself and your practices, and discuss anything the roommate may bring up besides rent payment.

Roommates also should want to avoid court for several reasons:

1. Public Records: If evicted, the record is now permanent and the record is public and can be searched

by other landlords. An eviction will appear on future tenant screens and may hamper their ability to obtain future housing. A non-court eviction is not registered in public databases unless the landlord seeks to identify places and makes the effort to file it themselves. I've never done that.

2. It will cost more: I place it in my lease that the roommate will pay court fees if they are evicted based on failure-to-pay. If a judgement is awarded and I can collect, it would include court fees.

3. Time and stress: it's certainly a lot less time, effort, funds and stress to not go to court.

F. <u>Use the security deposit as a bargaining chip</u>. One way to encourage your roommate to move out amicably is to consider offering a percentage of their security deposit if they move-out immediately and without damage. The possible return of their security deposit is your bargaining chip to gain compliance. A roommate hoping to reclaim a portion of their security deposit may encourage them to cooperate and keep your home undamaged during a hasty exit. This has worked for me.

- My story: my worst bozo cost me half the security deposit to convince him to move out quicker. There was no dispute that he hadn't paid his rent and owed other bills (i.e., phone charges, damages and theft), nor that he was insolvent and couldn't pay the bill; however, he planned not to move out till the last possible day. Waiting for a court ruling only extended the time he resided in my home and I also learned that it was illegal to lock him out. It is tougher to tolerate an undesirable tenant when they reside inside your personal dwelling. My attorney advised offering partial security refund if he moved immediately. My attorney also recommended I tell him his judgement would cost more adding court charges to the bill. He took the money-offer and moved out immediately. His quick exit meant he left a mess behind, but I preferred having him leave immediately verses tolerate his presence in my home awaiting a court eviction date. I had low expectations of collecting from him so getting him out allowed me to restore the unit sooner and not house him for free.

1. Overall rent is the largest problem and these recommendations are intended to help you structure a successful approach to collecting it! Next we'll discuss the other issues to consider before renting.

2. Cleanliness Policy: My experience is that nearly all of the roommates that read my *'Roommate Understanding''* expectations about cleanliness will generally comply; however, I've had the occasional messy roommate. Issues range from small pet-peeve issues to serious property damage. It's easy to say you want the premises kept in good clean condition but this needs to be defined!

   - My story #1: I've had two roommates cause significant property damages. The *"top-of-the-worst list"* was the bozo who cost more than his security deposit cleaning up the mess he created. I just told this story in the previous chapter under avoiding court using the security deposit refund. This roommate moved out but he left quickly and left behind a mess. Because I don't enter a roommate rental area, I didn't see any of the mess he had created beforehand. Upon entering his rooms I found these conditions:

- Rotten garbage and molding food. About 10 empty pizza boxes were pushed into the drawers and wardrobe closet while abandoned clothes where on the floor.

- The carpet was so heavily soiled it had to be removed.

- He ruined a new blanket by stuffing it into the windows as a curtain.

- The stove was so heavily soiled it required hours of professional cleaning.

- Trash of all kinds was strewn around, mostly onto the floor.

To deal with the mess, I hired a cleaning firm and incurred expenses beyond the value of having this roommate.

- My story #2: This roommate tried to be careful yet his job created unintentional damage.

  - An out-of-state contractor working on a ceramics contract didn't intentionally damage my property. The ceramics he worked with at his job were a powdery substance with a black residue. He carried a black-soot into the house which stained everything he touched. He helped attempt to wash soot off walls, doors, counters and the bathtub; however, it didn't wash out of the carpet, bedding or the uphol-stered couch. There was little I could have done to prevent this damage except understand his business and identify the issue sooner so I could cover non-washable items.

The first roommate did not pay for any of these damages but the second roommate covered costs to professionally clean the couch and carpet and helped clean the rest.

In contrast to these stories, most roommates did not cause severe damage and they also paid if damages occurred. Combined with a desire to get back a security deposit, clear expectations and respectful communications helped to avoid issues.

3. Guest Policy: In chapter 3, I discussed guest issues which include the number of visitors, overnight guests, noise, subletting, parties, and more you

allow? What will you do to set boundaries for these issues?

4. Noise Policy: It may be important to clarify what hours are quiet, volume of electronics, etc.

5. Security Policy: Clarify keys and copies of keys, securing windows, personal doors, house doors, etc.?

6. Access Policy: clarifying the space a roommate can use in the house and restricted areas.

7. Automobile Policy: Do you have specified or prohibited locations for parking? How many cars can they have? What about motorcycles? Is their car (or vehicles) in working condition? What about car noise (i.e., mufflers in disrepair?). Will you allow car repairs to be done on-site?

- My story: A roommate parked a disabled car on the street, planning to leave it there. The city ticketed, placed a warning sticker on it, and then towed it. She was pleased because they got rid of it for her! Another college student roommate drove an abused car whose old muffler got louder over time. Due to her financial situation I tolerated this and did not address it; however, eventually the police ticketed her, which prioritized having it repaired.

8. Storage Policy: Will you store items for your roommates?

9. Social Life Policy: Outline how social do you want to be with your roommates.

10. Utility cost recovery: Clarify how you are going to handle utilities and the roommate-portion.

11. A Written Expectations Outline: creating your *"Roommate Understanding"* agreement example. My *roommate expectations document* is fluid in that I regularly update it. Every time an issue occurs I add that issue to the document. I call my written expectations a *"Roommate Understanding"*. Below is an outline to create your own. Remember I give this document to prospective roommates in the interview phase and prior to signing a lease, and I attach it to the lease as a reminder. Elements to consider including in yours are:

RECOMMENDED WRITTEN
EXPECTATIONS COMPONENTS

1. Rent and late payments policy: You might begin with *"rent is due on the 1st day of the month and this is non-negotiable"* and outline your *"pay-to-stay"* relationship. Your late rent policy could then be outlined.

2. Eviction Issues: Besides not paying rent, there are a few issues that could be could result in eviction and then outline what these are for you.

3. List the other policies you want to communicate:

   • Restricted use house access

   • Kitchen policy

   • General cleanliness policy

   • Shared areas policy (i.e., laundry, garbage, porch)

- Guest policy

- Smoking policy

- Home security policy

- Utility policy

As stated in this book, I have had only a handful of bozo roommates who causes our housing relationship strain. Most individuals review these policies at the roommate interview and agree to them, even stating how much they appreciate the clarity and care spent communicating the expectations. I've found the document "roommate expectations" helps to attract the kind of person that appreciates similar clarity and will get along with me best, so I encourage you to design one that meets your needs.

CHAPTER 5 - The Money Room

ROOMMATE SCREENING

I have been grateful for my roommates. The experience was not problem-free and I've certainly has some hard lessons provided by my "bozos" roommates. I've learned to take care in selecting roommates and that I'd rather have no roommate than a bad one. This chapter provides advice and recommendations regarding roommate screening so you can avoid having a bozo of your own.

"Trust but verify" is a great motto in renting. I wish we could just believe that a person is who they say they are, that they pay their bills on-time, that they are clean, that they are financially solvent, and that they are generally honest, etc. Unfortunately, we have all met

someone who has not lived up to what they have told you about themselves. After some wrong first-impression experiences *"trust but verify"* became my underlying motto before allowing a stranger to move into my personal home. The most important thing I learned is <u>to always</u> perform a roommate screen!

1. Screening willingness is a good start: Someone that is willing to do the screening is the first sign they are OK and is more appealing as a potential roommate. Someone not wanting you to do a screen is a huge red flag. You are offering a non-traditional housing option and someone may be trying to avoid a traditional roommate screen because they cannot pass.

Even though I make it clear that I do a screening in all of my advertising, my property has attracted a couple people who tried to convince me not to do one. They either moved on when I insisted or I learned why a screen is essential:

- My story: One prospective roommate was a 35 year old man. He seemed very nice and his safety factor was heightened when his mother also attended the viewing appointment. He told me a believable story that he was separating from his wife and living in a hotel (that can be a bad sign). He stated several times he wanted the room as soon as possible to get out of the hotel, which sounded reasonable.

The first red flag was when he asked if I would waive the roommate screen because it would save money ($35). I held firm and stated *"no, I never waive this screen"*. He also asked if he could move in immediately, prior to completing the screen because he was "certain all would be fine". I resisted and reiterated I did the same process and screening for everyone and that the soonest a move-in had ever occurred was 48 hours, and only if I reached all his references timely.

He still completed the application and paid the $35.00 for the screening, probably hoping what I learned would not get revealed. I was shocked when the screen revealed that he had just been released from prison for his third heroin possession conviction, and even his three references I called confirmed he was an addict. When I called him to tell him I would not be taking him due to the criminal history, his response was *"I was falsely accused, the heroin wasn't mine; it belonged to friends who left it in my car"*. My response was *"I'm sorry but I can't take someone who has three convictions or friends' with heroin"*.

From this story a few lessons were clear. The first lessons learned was I can make a bad first impression. Secondly I learned that someone might try to con me or at least not be fully honest. The most important lesson I learned was to always do a roommate screen and even more so if the prospective roommate tries to talk me out of it!

2. Screening Permission: Did you know you need a prospective roommate's permission first before you screen? Most landlords do this in the form of a signed application. The application provides a signature at the bottom giving explicit permission to submit the signed application as screening consent. This is at the end of my application:

Applicant Signature _____

Today's Date _ _ _ / _ _ _ / _ _ _ _

(Your signature provides authorization for screening, including any agency running a traditional Roommate Screen for criminal, credit + eviction history)

The prospective roommate must provide personal information to do the screening including a driver's license and a social security number. Having the applicant's identification up-front when communication is friendly is useful if things go bad; you'd have their identification to file court forms and later find them if debt-collection is needed.

3. Establishing legitimacy: Landlord's need to document legitimacy before being able to order a tenant screen. Before you can purchase a screen you need prove you are a landlord. You can do this multiple ways including:

A. Using your Federal I.D. (i.e., in the USA a personal society security number) and documenting the income on a Schedule C of your tax return.

B. Establishing your business with your state and being issued a business E.I.N. government tax/ business ID.

C. Establishing LLC provides the legitimacy; however it is much more involved. I'll discuss this in a later chapter.

4. Roommate Screening Sources: I recommend you get both credit check and background check services. Ways to obtain a credit screen include:

A. Apartment Associations can be invaluable as they always have a relationship with a screening firm that will work with all association members no matter what their size. This is important when you have only a one or few units. In my State of Ohio, laws changed and landlords needed to offer 10+ units to get full screening privileges. Homeowner-landlords can leverage an Apartment Association membership as credibility and get the same access to a reputable screening company. You might also get preferred screening rates through your apartment association.

B. Web Pages – many sources provide screen ing services. Some are as low as $19.99 but investigate if what they provide is what you need? There are online websites which allow you to find your intended person quickly and easily. One site suggested the top 10 Background Check companies are (FYI this is unverified by the authors personal use as I never used any of these sites):

- RoommateBackgroundSearch.com -- https://www.roommatebackgroundsearch.com/

- TransUnionSmartMove.com - https://www.mysmartmove.com/

- Checkmate.com - http://www.instant-checkmate.com/?src=NNEE&mdm=NET-WORK&cmp=NNEE&cnt=B467XIXS65&affi-d=38&campid=112&sid=NNEE&s1=B467XIX-S65&s2=&s3=&lp=%2F

- BeenVerified.com- http://www.top10bestback-groundcheck.com/visit.php?site=BeenVeri-fied&bidata={%22slb%22:996745,%22sr%22:null,%22blrsc%22:1040476,%22blrs%22:1236}

- American Apartment Owners Association (does roommate screening). http://www.amer-ican-apartment-owners-association.org/best-credit-report-10/?utm_source=bing&utm_me-dium=cpc&utm_campaign=Roommate%20 Screening%20Campaign%20-%20Search%20 Opt&utm_term=roommate%20screening&utm_content=Roommate%20screening

- Lease Runner. https://www.leaserunner.com/roommate-screening-services

There are plenty more and I advise you review the site reputation before using it. I preferred using a local company referred by the apartment association.

5. Paying the Screening Company: I recommend you find a screening company that does not have a membership fee, sign-up fee, minimum orders or usage, or monthly service charges.

- My story: I use a company that does one time/one-fee screen and recommended by the apartment association. I suggest you charge the prospective roommate the fee as it proves legitimate interest before proceeding. I share the report with the roommate as they paid for it.

6. Screening content: What kinds of things will the screen provide and things to consider? This will vary by your State and the laws. In my State of Ohio because I have under 10 units roommate screeners can only provide a report that says "recommended/approve" or "reject" without the details. It's more like a pass/fail report. Landlords with more than 10 units can get a full-report.

7. Red Flags: What *red flags* or "concerning indicators" should you be on the lookout; what items might indicate a problem roommate potential?

A. Low credit score and type-of-debt history: A low score alone is not an indicator; however my Apartment Association recommended that you look at the type of debts. If they do not pay the things that they must have to live (i.e., utilities) then this may mean they have trouble paying day-to-day expenses. This also may mean they will have trouble paying your bills. If the debts are non-living expenses (i.e., medical debts) this may indicate credit issues were the result of unplanned life-issues and less about day-to-day expenses and this is less of an issue. If you see unpaid utility, phone and rent history, then you have a legitimate concern they will continue to not pay these bills with you.

B. Criminal history: Most sites state they have access to hundreds of millions of national and statewide criminal records. Some cite America's Most Wanted, FBI's Most Wanted, and the National Sex Offender Registry. You may want to investigate if the screening covers the entire USA or just one state. Because the person will be in my home, I have chosen to not take anyone with any kind of criminal history outside of a traffic violation.

C. Multiple recent past addresses: You might want to consider it a red flag if the report shows frequent moves and multiple addresses. If someone moves often and has stays less than 1 year at locations, it becomes a red flag. You might have a conversation about the problem or issue that caused them to move? People getting evicted often move a lot. You should require a good answer to questions about the reason behind frequent moves. There could be good reasons too (i.e., moved for jobs, family, military, etc.). Frequent moves due to eviction are often accompanied by debts in other categories.

D. An eviction report: It may be possible to run a former landlord search. Unfortunately the landlord data-base is not comprehensive as these data bases are voluntary, not linked together, and few landlords have participated. Because of this if you identify a negative, take it seriously as these data-base searches are usually only from the *'big players'* and any negative is a good indication you have a roommate with a renting problem.

8. Screening substitutes: An employment screen might be better than what a landlord can obtain because they can do drug and deeper reference checks. If the roommate-candidate clears the more rigorous company screening and their Human Resources department will verify that with me, I accept that HR written verification and not repeat that part of the screen-

ing process. This has never proven a bad decision. I still conduct a reference check (discussed next). Corporate Human Resources department professionals can do a more thorough roommate verification than landlords because they can also obtain education verifications, employee references, criminal screening and often a drug screening.

9. Make your own reference check calls: This is one way to hear whether or not people like this potential roommate and increase your comfort-level considering their application. You should make the following calls:

A. Employee Verification: If you are not already working with the HR Department on a roommate screening per above, you should verify employment. This is very easy; just call the prospective roommates' company and ask if they work there. For legal reasons the company is not allowed to tell you much else.

B. Former landlord reference verification: this can be an extremely important screening tool. The most important questions are:

- Did they pay their rent?

- Did they pay on time? and

- Someone told me the most a reference can legally say is '*whether or not they would rent to them again*", so ask them "*would you rent to them again*"?

In my experience if the roommate was great, the landlord will add compliments. If not they may add nothing more than the first two question answers but might add good comments if the person was a great tenant.

C. Three character reference calls: The prospective roommate's personal references is the last step to determine if the person is an amicable match to your preferences and lifestyle. There are two obvious flaws with personal references: 1). the person will provide only the best character references, and 2) the person could have provide references that they've known only a short time. The less time the reference has known he person, the less credible the reference will be about the person.

- My story: I learned to consider the length of time the references knew the person through my experience because my worst bozo roommate (the same person that left my home a mess, ran up the phone bill, and I had to pay to move out). Provided all his references from people he'd known at his job for three weeks. In hindsight perhaps he didn't have stronger, longer-known references because of his character issues. After that experience I'd ask the person to provide me someone in addition that has known them longer.

In making your reference calls there are legal limitations regarding the questions you can ask and what the reference can legally tell you. Your questions must comply with fair-housing laws and be non-discriminatory. I strongly advise you ask open-ended questions that invite the person to tell you information and then just listen. The quieter and longer you can be silent, the more they might tell you about the person. I ask these questions after giving a brief overview of my reason for calling:

i) How long have you known the prospective roommate?

ii) If you were me, would you let this prospective roommate live with you?

iii) Is there anything else you think I should know about the prospective roommate?

- Another story: Of course I prefer to accept roommate candidates who get glowing references. I begin to feel very comfortable taking candidates when their references tell me things like '*what a great person they are*' and how much they are liked. I did once have a candidate whose references told me "*well, they are known to have an anger problem*" and in response to my second question above two references answered "*no, I wouldn't rent to them myself*". I didn't take that person.

10. Example Roommate Application content: Below is my rental application content, including a signature approval for a screening.

A. Disclaimer: This application is NOT a Rental Agreement. This application is preliminary only and does not obligate the homeowner to execute a

Lease. This application assumes that the applicant is of legal age and will meet the financial obligations of an executed Lease. Further, the applicant has received and has read the "Rental Understanding" and agrees to abide by this "Understanding" for successful roommate cohabitation.

B. Sample content to include in your application:

1. PRINT   First   Name _____ MI _____

   Last _____

2. How to reach you: phone, email

3. Present address: _____

4. Social Security # ___ ___ ___ - ___ ___ - ___ ___ ___ ___ (needed for the roommate screen)

5. DOB _ _ / _ _ / _ _   Driver's Lic. # _ _ _ _ _ _ _ _ _ _ _ _ State _____ (needed for the roommate screen)

6. Employment Verification: Present Employer

7. Present Apartment or Landlord

8. Landlord's Phone and reason for moving?

9. Employment Verification: Present Employer and the company's phone and contact

10. Gross Monthly Income $_____

11. How long have you been with the company (could be new). Since: _ _ / _ _ / _ _

C. References, provide at least three who will verify you would be a good roommate

Leave space for 3-entries.

D. Relevant credit details for supporting ability to pay rent and be a good roommate: (If yes for any, provide the details on a separate page):

- Have you ever broken a Lease? Yes / No

- Have you ever been evicted? Yes / No

- Are you illegal drug free: Yes / No

- Have you ever been convicted of a felony? Yes / No

- Have you had a collection action taken against you in the past 3 years? yes/ No

- Have you ever filed bankruptcy, garnished wages

or been sued for non-payment of rent or damages to rental property? Yes / No

E. VEHICLE - List the type of Vehicle to be parked on the premises (car, truck, van). Note: there is only room for one vehicle per roommate and no disabled ones.

F. EMERGENCY INFORMATION-- Do you have any medial issues for which the homeowner should be informed: Yes / No

- If yes, provide the details on a separate page.

- Contact in case of a medical issue or emergency

G. Applicant Signature _____
Today's Date __ /___ /__

(Your officials signature provides authorization for screening, including any agency running a traditional Roommate Screen for criminal, credit + eviction history)

In conclusion, the moral of this chapter, no matter how much you initially like or want to believe someone, it's better to always *"trust first but then verify"*.... All my roommate regrets came from overlooking roommate screen red flags.

CHAPTER 6 - The Money Room

ADVERTISING & FINDING ROOMMATES

There are many ways to find roommates and it's usually through trial-and-error that you will find what works best for you. I'll share recommendations you might choose, but your experience may differ from mine. In speaking with other landlords I've learned most use a combination of approaches work to attract roommates.

1. Referrals and word-of-mouth first: You might start by telling friends and family, and creating a network of people through work, church and your personal life. While I've found roommates this way only twice, your experience could be more re-warding. You might develop an email list of those

who express interest in helping (such as family, friends, contacts at church, workplace, etc.). Include former roommates as they are your best reference. Utilize social networking (i.e., Facebook) to inform about the property.

2. Internet Advertising: There are plenty of online roommate sites: to help people find roommates. I prefer Craigslist. There's Roommate.com, Sublet.com, EasyRoommate; Roommate2Go; Uloop; and Zillow and other similar sources. I recommend sticking to those that are roommate-specifically because Zillow and Sublet does not have a housemate category.

I prefer Craigslist. After failing to identify a roommate through the local contacts, I place a Craigslist advertisement. I like Craigslist for these reasons:

A. There's a lot of space for a complete advertisement. Below I demonstrate how much information I can place in a Craig's list ad.

Craig's List Ad Example

A professional offers a home-share to an INDIVID-UAL ROOMMATE (one person only) in a very CLEAN suburban home on the border of ___x___. Rent is $__x. xx__ month including full-furnishings and INCLUDING most utilities (internet but not phone or cable). Short-term 3 month leases + month-to-month after. Room-mates have stayed 4 months to 5 years.

Rent FULLY-FURNISHED separate private rooms! This 1-bedroom "apartment" is the lower-level of a home that features a separate entrance and four furnished separate rooms (a Living Room, private bathroom with shower-only, bedroom, and a kitchenette) similar to a residence-hotel but costs much less (the closest residence hotel runs $900 month minimum).

This property is also strictly smoke-free.

The house is kept very clean and roommate cleanliness is required.

SCREENING PROCESS: We begin with a phone discussion, then a showing appointment, then complete an application process. Move-in requires a rental application and a reference-security review (takes at least 2 weeks to complete roommate check before move-in). The screening application costs include a $35 fee for roommate screen via the __xx__Screen Co. There is one other option: if the prospective roommate's human-resources department works with the landlord to verify in writing/email/phone that they completed a drug+criminal+security screening and they will provide written documentation, then that part of the screening can be replaced with theirs.

TO INVESTIGATE: telephone to begin the process at this number _____. My name.

If you include a phone number, you will need to encode it using a combination of printed numbers so that scanning bots cannot get your phone number. Use a combination of numbers and spelling such as two-3–four, 11two zero, etc. Finally I note in the advertisement that the number is a land-line and no texting possible. I prefer calls to go to an answering machine verses my cell phone so I can respond at my convenience.

B. Craigslist helps with screening: Craig's List eliminates several issues that come with newspaper advertising due to the ability to provide detailed information stating what you are renting, pictures of the rental area, a location map, and more importantly, rental expectations. A Craigslist ad begins the screening process.

C. Craig's List has a national audience. There are people I would have never reached had I not advertised on Craigslist that turned out to be awesome roommates including these roommates two roommate stories:

- Tim the computer-guru worked four-months as a computer contractor for a local manufacturer. Tim was a married man from Tennessee who initially reached out to me while housed temporarily at a local hotel. He preferred a home situation verses the hotel for his 4-month contract. We had a mutually respectful friendship and I became a housing reference for him when he went on to repeat the experience in new locations.

- My favorite roommate was Patrick the Navy Seal, a married former military man with two-young children back home. His one-year contract performing medical equipment repair at the Veterans Administration Hospital brought him to the area. He worked long hours for three weeks and then went home once per-month to visit his family. His military world-view and laid-back sense of humor provided for lively conversations whenever we encountered each other. I also benefited bartering for home repairs and odd jobs (i.e., hauling air-conditioners). When he returned home, we continued to exchange email and stay in touch.

D. One negative: Craigslist advertising does generate spam email. While annoying it's not a deal-breaker. There is a significant increase in junk email and phishing attempts immediately following placing a Craigslist advertisement; however these fake-responses are both easily identifiable and deleted. Once you place an ad you will receive dozens of auto-emails that are not legitimate roommate candidates but someone trying to get you to provide personal information, presumably for scamming purposes. These responses are easy to identify because they follow a pattern:

- They generally begin by asking about rental, often so general you can see it is not a direct response to your ad. Some say about your *"room-apartment-home"* and are obviously casting a wide-net to include your type of rental.

- They ask basic questions about your rental which you clearly stated in your ad (i.e., how much is it?)

- They often tell a generalized story about relocating to your area, usually from another Country

- They offer unsolicited personal comments about what a great person they are, generally things that would be appealing in a real roommate such as *"I am clean, I am quiet"*, etc.

- They move quickly and suggest immediately moving-in and ask for you to hold the room for them.

- They always end by asking you to send them personal information. They encourage you to send your address and bank account so they can send you a deposit.

I assume the worst -- the email is some kind of scam seeking to get my address for invasive reasons and I delete it, moving-on to legitimate responders.

If at first you do not recognize one of these spam emails and you respond, it won't harm you. Within seconds you will get back a second email that is more of the same asking you to go to the next step and send your personal contact information and bank account. Another clear sign it is spam is that their email addresses change; the first email and second are not the same.

The main way to differentiate a real email from the spam is that the legitimate email will provide a phone number to call you, or start the process by calling you. If you do email, the email is going to come from an email supplier you recognize and the exchange will continue through that same email. These are good initial signs the respondent is legitimate and not a spammer.

3. Local Businesses: I've had success working with local corporations. One major advantage of working with a local company is that H.R. departments perform even more extensive screening than landlords can access.

My story: I identified a niche market with local corporations. After introducing myself to Human Resources managers at local companies, I ended up establishing a long-term relationship with one company that lasted over 10 years. Their HR manager recruited college students and also managed housing for relocating professionals. This company found my housing option perfect because I offered a *'fully-furnished property"* and a *"short-term lease option'*, and further my property cost 1/2 as much as the closest residence hotel. Finally my property was less than a mile from their facility.

Every single roommate they sent was a beneficial symbiotic relationship. This firm kept my units occupied with at least one roommate for more than 10 years. Their college student interns were carefully selected young people with bright minds and bright careers. They proved to be great young people that were always respectful, hard-working young professionals with promising careers ahead of them. Some were pretty interesting characters too.

- One student was from Jordan and played a sitar; some pretty unique sounds emanated from his rooms at night.

- Another student was from Lebanon and we frequently discussed cultural differences

- One student made beer on weekends and sometimes the strong flavors, such as pumpkin, filled the house!

I was very disappointed when economic circumstances caused them to disband the program. Obviously I identified a truly niche market and benefited from an ideal symbiotic relationship providing housing for this corporate client.

A quote from one of these roommates:

"Sharing the house temporarily with Michelle was easy and affordable. I was able to come and go as I needed. It offered all I needed, such as a clothes washer and drier conveniently located in the home, and more than enough room to keep my "stuff".

Steve B.

4. Local college or schools: If you have one nearby that attracts out-of-state students, they have a housing department that helps students identify housing options. Each one approaches it individually so you should work with their Housing Department to access their system. Sometimes they allow campus fliers but you generally have to work with an on-campus office for approval and postings are short-term.

5. Niche marketing: The possibilities are endless to identify markets where your specialize attracting a specific clientele. Finding a niche market helps to focus your property advertising to meet your needs and stand out from competitor options. Some of the thoughts I had for niche markets that might find home-rental appealing:

A. College students: if your property close to a large college, or any training program that attracts out-of-area students, they often have a student housing department. They sometimes advertise off-campus housing.

B. Seniors: can you offer rental services to a seniors? You can try advertising at city senior centers or aging associations.

C. Relocation support: If you are willing to provide a housing alternative for families-in-transition, you could work with realtors.

D. Hospital employees: If you are near a hospital, you might rent to interns who will be in the area for 1-2 years needing temporary rental. Hospitals might even help you advertise in their own housing webpage

E. Local program provider, ministry or transitional housing provider: These groups often need transitional housing providers. They have both funding sources and can screen the candidates. They may also contribute towards the housing bill.

F. People with housing needs can found through funded programs. For instance I've been contacted by programs helping the mentally challenged, young people aging out of the system, young mothers, etc.

G. Handicapped/disabled housing provider: If you are willing to install handicapped accessories and provide adapted housing, there's a large population needing independent housing. If you are close to a medical facility, can identify available handicap transportation options (i.e., specialized bus line services), you have a ready group seeking housing options. An expert tells me there are other issues to investigate (i.e., such as special licensure) so if you are interested in this, contact your local disability association or senior center to learn what is involved.

6. Posting a flier in local businesses: You might post a flier/ad in local businesses such as local coffee house type places that have a public posting area churches, grocery stores, libraries, and other local businesses near your home. I created a half page flier that advertised a fully-furnished rental and placed them around town.

7. Newspaper ads: This is an option if you can attract rental candidates through simplistically worded ads. Certainly it provides a large outreach in your

local city. Personally, I had trouble with the newspaper advertising due to both ad brevity and cost. For me it was an inefficient recruiting source. What contributed to my issues that will need to consider are:

A. Cost: Because newspaper advertisement is charged per line, I tried to keep it as short as possible. My ad was three lines even when short and abbreviated. The ad costs more if run on weekends. For instance, the advertisement below cost $40.50 to run for just one weekend in a local newspaper.

B. Ad Brevity: The biggest issue is the shortness of the ad due to cost and space, so you are limited to few words which means that the prospective reader doesn't know enough about your property. My ad read as this: Share Nice/CLEAN house in Euclid. Pvt BR, BA, LR, Kit, $500+Sec, xxx-xxx-xxxx Due to the ad brevity, the responses attracted people who didn't want what I was offering and the advertisement brevity didn't screen for these issues:

1. Fully-furnished: many applicants were disqualified due to having furniture.

2. Reference checks: I've had inquiring callers hang up as soon as they heard I performed a screening.

3. No pets: I had callers seeking housing allowing a pet. Upon learning I had cats, occasionally a caller would state that they hated cats or had allergies.

4. Ref+Sec: while the paper allowed an abbreviation for references and security, there wasn't enough space to cite the amount. I had people hang up when they learned the security deposit amount and that I was non-negotiable about it.

5. Single person only: Due to fair housing laws, the newspaper wouldn't let me include this content due to publisher fair-housing laws. The newspaper would not let me print that I was seeking a roommate or individual person either. It caused me to receive numerous calls from couples and people with children.

6. Minimum 3-month: not including this issue caused people looking for AIRNUB and hotel one-

night stays which I do not offer.

7. Lower level unit: I had a woman in a wheelchair who called every time the advertisement ran who liked the rent price but struggled to understand that there were 13 steep steps to navigate and that the rental was not wheelchair accessible.

8. Not near bus line: I had callers without personal transportation and had to spend time discussing that the closest bus stop was over a 1.5 miles away. My home is not near public transportation.

In summary, not being able to state the issues above attracted people who were not interested in what I was offering and I had to take time eliminating these unqualified callers.

C. The newspaper circulation range: the more distant the paper distribution from your home the more limited the response. It works better if you use a small and local newspaper with community-character for your advertising.

The above demonstrates many issues raised from an advertisement short and simplistic. IF you do decide to try newspaper ads, my recommendation is to advertise only on the weekends. The people who read weekdays are also weekend readers. Advertising only on weekends will save you paying for the same readers.

In conclusion, I've had the most success with Craigslist and it is my main source of advertising if my local efforts do not succeed. Everyone has to find their approach to identifying quality roommates and I hope my suggestions guide your choices.

CHAPTER 7 - The Money Room

TAXES AND LEGAL AND MORE

Last chapter! I'm assuming you have now decided to pursue having a roommate, have made decisions regarding your home and rental offering, your lease, your expectations and your advertising. Let's cap-off your planning efforts reviewing legal issues, tax advantages, and whether or not you should set up an official business entity.

Legal Issues: Roommate laws are fewer and less difficult than regular non-resident landlord rules. Because it's your home you have more choices; however, it is still worth it to investigate local and legal rental rules.

1. Apartment Association assistance: Landlord associations exist throughout the United States and may in other countries. These associations provide you many positive things:

   A. Provides legitimacy to your small business. You can leverage an association membership to assist with your rental credibility, get advice and network with support and services.

   B. Roommate Screen company: They can help you get access to a reputable screening company. Association membership also gains your small rental business legitimacy despite having less than 10 units, a typical minimum for many screening companies.

   C. Networking: They provide networking opportunities with other landlords.

   D. Contacts within the city, and often experiences and advice dealing with your city and court system.

   E. Training and information. My associations offered a "Fair Housing Law" training so I avoided making mistakes in this area. They may also provide you lease and document samples, support creating your lease, eviction support, advertising advice, viewing approaches, and other rental advice.

F. Discounts with businesses that support landlords such as paint, carpet, cleaning etc.

2. Investigate your city and state rental rules:

A. State resources: depending on your age, you may remember that investigating meant a trip to the library or even the courthouse. Sometimes this material is still found in the library and depending on your City it may be online. A place to start is your state webpage and type in "landlord or property rental" and other similar wording. Each state has their own legislated rental process (i.e., leases, eviction).

B. City office: I recommend approaching your building department and asking questions as a 'landlord' but explain you are renting rooms. You might introduce yourself to the local building inspector and discuss roommate rental issues.

My city requires all landlords do an annual property inspection looking at exits, fire alarms and extinguishers; however, for an on-site property owner with a roommate no inspection was required. They recommended I provide fire alarms and have fire extinguishers in the kitchens, otherwise they didn't require inspections for a home-owner occupied property.

C. Information and research sources:

- An Apartment Association

- Your local library: I found a couple books-on-tape there were very helpful.

- Web Pages – many sources aexist. For instance, I have posted educational blogs at **www. TheMoneyRoomBook.com.**

3. Tax advantages: One of the advantages of having a home-based business is that it helps reduce the expenses of owning a home and reduces your tax liability against the added income. It's ironic that your rental home-based business is also the rental. Here

are some suggestions to help you gain tax deductions:

A. Consider hiring a Certified Public Accountant (CPA).. If you do your own taxes, you will need to understand rental laws. A CPA is up-to-date on law changes and deduction possibilities, so I turn this over to CPA expertise. My CPA identified additional deductions and completed taxes faster due to her experience. It's important to remember your tax preparation fee includes future defense of your tax submission should you be audited.

B. Deductions: You can deduct a percentage of all your home costs. Here's how to calculate the deduction amount. It is a percentage of the rental use vs. your personal house use. You identify the amount of your complete home's space vs. the rental space percentage within the home. To review this another way::

- Determine the total square footage of your home

- Determine the % of your home that is room-mate space (a deductible expenses %)

- Determine the % of your home that is dedicated office space (a deductible expenses %)

- Once you figure out the percentage of your house being used for the business, this is the percent deducted from all your expenses.

C. Deductions include:

- Common area improvements

- Roommate specific expenses (i.e., things bought exclusively for the rental unit).

- A percentage of all house costs including utilities, insurance, maintenance, repairs, etc.

- Office expenses: % of your printer, computer, stamps, paper, envelopes, etc. that are used in your business office.

4. Documentation: I recommend you create a documentation system so that you can demonstrate legitimate deductions. It's suggested you keep the records for seven years in case of an audit. The things you should consider recording:

A. Rent documentation. I create a single Excel spreadsheet for the roommate income. I dually use it as for the CPA and the roommate. For the CPA, I tally the income at the end-of-year as the rental documentation.

B. Files for the related deductions (i.e., utilities, office supplies, insurance, maintenance, roommate specific expenses). Drop all receipts into these files to support your expenses.

5. Separate banking: For tax clarity my CPA recommended having a separate checking and business credit card to clearly document and separate business expenses. I opened a separate checking account which held rents, security deposit holding and expenses payments. I also obtained a business credit card used for roommate and home expenses and paid these expenses using the rent money. This creates a separate expense and income tracking system not mixed in with personal finances. This makes things easier for the accountant and serves as your tax documentation/proof.

6. Attorney recommendations: If things go wrong, you may need to consult an attorney. I use a pre-paid legal service called <u>Legal Shield</u> that costs less annually than many lawyers charge hourly (as of this printing, $17.95 per month), and a home-business rider is another $10.00 per month to handle your business issues. This service has been invaluable helping me each time I had issues.

Legal Shield reviewed my lease and other legal forms (i.e., application, 3-day eviction notice, eviction warning) and provided advice (i.e., eviction questions). Every time I've called they respond within 24-hours. I recommend arranging for a pre-paid legal service to assist you if you do not have an attorney. If you want to check out Legal Shield go to this webpage <u>www.michellebrady.legalshieldassociate.com</u>. I've set up representing Legal Shield because I have benefited from them so much. Full disclosure, I do make a few dollars if you join but that's not the reason I promote them. I'm convinced they will be a great asset to anyone venturing into rental, with the first task of helping you create your lease.

7. Considering a LLC: The main reason to consider a separate entity is liability. A LLC means Limited Liability Corporation, which is a business structure that separates your personal and business assets. It protects you in case a roommate sued you (i.e., someone falling, theft, fire or other issues). If you have a LLC, the suit could only encompass the assets the business owns and not your personal assets. This is especially important if you own other property or assets. An attorney can advise you if you should consider a LLC or not.

- My story: Initially I did not get an LLC because I had few assets. At that time, I reported my roommate income on a tax form called a Schedule C. As I developed a retirement fund and savings, I considered ensuring that my business assets and personal assets were separate. Setting--up an LLC is a relatively easy and inexpensive. I worked with an attorney to establish the LLC paperwork ($200) and filed with my State (about $100). I was issued an EIN number and my little business was officially a formal business entity. Nothing changed except that the business is legally separated and the tax forms are more involved. I pay my CPA slightly more to file the business taxes. I was assured by others in the business that this protection gives peace-of-mind and I wouldn't lose personal assets to a roommate suit.

The Money Room

Conclusion

Thank you for the honor sharing your time to read my book. It was my hope that my experiences helped you navigate renting, avoid pitfalls and create your own great roommate success stories.

It would be a privilege to support you in other ways than this book. I also offer:

- Training: I can present through phone, interviews, key-note presentations, and half and full-day workshop formats.

- Blog updates: topical articles will be offered online and you can follow my blog at **www.TheMoney-RoomBook.com**.

- Personal Coaching: individual support as you navigate renting.

- Share your story with me and possibly readers: Contact me and share your experiences, opinions, suggestions, advice and insights. You can email me at <u>MBrady@SageForward.com</u>.

I wish you the best sharing your home with a roommate, and as I said about my house in the first page: *"may your home never be lonely."*

CPSIA information can be obtained
at www.ICGtesting.com
Printed in the USA
LVOW03s0848100418
572852LV00003B/4/P

9 781628 654387